Dedication,

To my dear readers, I dedicate this book to all those who have faced the hardships of displacement, forced migration, and the uncertainty of starting anew Life.

To my fellow refugees, may this book serve as a testament to our resilience and strength in the face of adversity.

To those who have never experienced the challenges of being a refugee, may this book offer a glimpse into our world and inspire empathy and compassion, may it remind us of all that behind every statistic and news headline, there are real human beings with stories, dreams, and hopes for a better future.

I also dedicate this book to all the individuals and organizations who work tirelessly to support refugees and promote their rights, your dedication and compassion give us hope and make our journey a little easier.

Lastly, I dedicate this book to my family, who have been my rock and my motivation throughout this journey, without their love and support, I would not be where I am today.

Thank you for reading and for being a part of my journey.

Introduction

In a world where culture and tradition define one's worth and success, a family of six struggles to break free from the shackles of their societal expectations, As they navigate the pressures of education and the pursuit of their dreams, they come face to face with the harsh reality of financial constraints and the fear of the unknown. Join them on their journey of self-discovery as they grapple with the decision to leave behind everything they have ever known in search of a better life, and the consequences that follow   This is a story about the power of familial love, the strength of individual ambition, and the courage it takes to break free from the status quo.

Table of Contents

Extract 1, The Family's struggle's & dreams.

An African Family Of 6 they had 4 kids they lived a decent yet vulnerable life, Their dad was never around because he was always working & takes as much extra shifts as he possibly can to provide for them an education and life, their mum on the other hand was only a high school graduate & only spoke Arabic, yet she managed to teach them a language she doesn't master.

English was the language they took pride in, their dad had titles set for them set since they were little, Asala is a Dr, Aseel is a pilot, Asail is an engineer & Asool is a teacher,

Their whole lives were based on the thought of these children growing up, fulfilling their Parents dreams to becoming respectable, presentable individuals,

A lot of it was the cultural pressure and the collective consciousness behind the idea, if my child does not identify or is labelled as a Dr, Teacher, or Engineer, its simply isn't satisfying enough.

A child without education is like a bird without wings Said their father on regular basis.

Their Father made sure they entered the best schools, Learnt the most international language. *"ENGLISH"*

Some even though they spoke English before a proper word of Arabic.

With a few Members of the Family against it, under the claims, the English language is not important,

The English language would interfere with their thoughts & the way they were meant to be shaped, Under the claims that this path of Education brings more harm than good

Their Father disagreed,

> *I will make sure it became a part of these children, My Children Says their father.*

He saw hopes & dreams perhaps his own portrayed in these Children.

As Seasons went by, these children were growing & becoming Young Adults & as much beauty that holds, along came responsibilities & the urge to have the Future ready for them, the urge to provide intensifies & becomes a Burden for these Parents.

Life doesn't seem to go as planned suddenly all these savings & hard work wasn't enough, Higher education is costly very costly for one man's shoulder...

> *Let's get out of here,*
>
> *Let's see what lies beyond this land,*
>
> *Let's get out of here,*
>
> *Let's see what's beyond these planes & their destinations, says their Eldest Says Asala*

Oddly, The First to Support those quests was Her Mother.

In all probability, their Mother thought anywhere beyond Africa Represented Freedom.

I have been stuck in this side of the world that profess Love & kindness but it's not says their mother.

I am tired of this life that lacks stability, says their mother.

Despite these Parents always being on the same page they seem to have a divided opinion,

do we leave everything we knew behind? do we leave Family?

Do we leave the culture we knew & grew up with, do we leave this life we created in the hands of the unknown says their father?

With every day getting harder, the thought of a better life out there sinks in their fathers' thoughts.

 As Days & Months goes by after asking around for direction on what is the right steps to be done to get to that better life.

Right, Let's start applying for Visas says their father.

As they put all their savings & head to almost every European Governmental representative with every rejection bestowed upon them, they become more eager & there it is... Human nature.

But what would come next for the family?

Could they finally be able to achieve their dream of a better life abroad? Or would they face even more obstacles and challenges along the way?

Only time will tell.

Extract 2, The journey begins.

The word gets around, this family is seeking a pathway to the other side.

A stranger appeared,

I can help, I can show you the way out, I can promise you to make your life better, says the stranger, claiming he has the way out under his fingertips.

Hesitant, confused, and anxious become the father for all those pillow talks with his partner about going forward with this, feels close & real.

Let's do this, says their father.

What do you need from me? says the father to this stranger.

Quoting a large amount per person, says the stranger!

As Both ends came to an agreement, despite the hesitation & the worry that their father tries to hide,

I am not sure what to call this stranger, a stranger? A human smuggler? A thief? A salesman pitching a bargain, "better life" says their father.

I am not sure what to call myself a father, or an irresponsible father.

I am not sure if I am a good father anymore!

Do I still get to call myself a father? says these children's father in hesitation!

As the deal was made, the agreements were established, and the day has come, They were sent a location by the beach.

Get your things ready, don't grab more than you can carry, says their mother.

We are leaving, leaving and not looking back, says their mother.

Why? How? Are you sure about this? says their eldest Asala?

No questions asked, just do what I say, says the mother.

The location was across the other side.

Great Egypt, where their journey really begins. or was the journey already started the day they thought about leaving?

Arriving to the location given, Who are these people, who are these men, women, children waiting onshore?

Could they possibly be coming along with us? says the children amongst themselves?

Get on the boat, hold each other's hands!" yells a stranger.

From standing still questioning themselves, the location, this decision, in a matter of seconds, rushing into the water to get on this small boat alongside others.

As The beauty of sunrise is breathtaking as the sky gradually shifts from dark to a warm hue of orange and pink, bringing the promise of a new day and a fresh start.

The first rays of sunlight peek over this boat & onboard people with different backgrounds yet the same dream

We arrived, we arrived! yells the stranger on the boat.

Arrived where? says these children's father alongside other people.

To a bigger ship, This will get us to reach our destination," says this stranger as he helped everyone onto the ship.

Following his words, everyone on this boat gets onto the ship.

Are we desperate refugees huddled together, seeking a better life on a creaky ship? Says their eldest Asala.

From this point onward, are we travellers? Are we survivors? Or do we just identify as people on holidays, and this is just a cruise? thought Asala, stranded in the vast expanse of water and sky, with no sign of land in sight,

The promise was four days to reach Europe!

Why are we still here? asks the children to their parents.

We are almost there, claims the mother to her children.

Days after days under the harsh sun & the cold at night, as the ship rode the crest of each wave, the creaking and groaning of its timbers echoed through the air, while the panicked cries of the passengers grew louder with each passing moment.

Their faces etched with terror as they braced themselves for the next jarring impact & yet as calm as a great mother would be, "We are almost there" she says.

As the days went by, the water supply began to dwindle, and the passengers became increasingly worried.

As the days went by, the water supply began to dwindle, and the passengers became increasingly worried, the family of six had been rationing their water, but they too were down to their last bottle.

Their mother knew she had to do something to help her children, one step ahead of everyone else on that ship, she kept the last bottle of water and cautiously poured it into the bottle's cap for each one of her children's dry mouths.

Enough is enough, said Asala to the sky and the power she thought rests behind it.

Desperation in her eyes was palpable as she stared up at the endless blue sky, silently wishing for it all to end.

Just as they were about to succumb to their fate, a miracle happened.

The sound of a helicopter rotor could be heard in the distance, growing louder and louder.

As the refugees looked up, they saw a bright red and white Italian marine helicopter swooping down towards them.

Extract 3, Angelic beings.

They were all dressed in white, Angelic beings thought Asala.

Little did she know that their uniforms were meant to protect them from any diseases that may have been present on the ship from passengers, these passengers from the third world countries.

The Marines helped everyone onto their enormous ship, and Asala and her siblings were among the first to go.

However, when she sat down to drink water, she noticed that her father was not with among the people getting into the ship, The Marines had a policy of women and children first but even after the wait, there was still no sign of her father.

Asala asked around and was told that a man was helping offload people from the ship, and she knew it was her father, She wasn't surprised, He always puts himself last, selfless Man.

how disturbing, this is not the time for it, Says Asala in anger to her mother.

As the Marines began distributing food and water, Asala & her siblings amongst others ate proper food for the first time in 10 days.

She heard a Soldier trying to communicate with one of her fellow refugees as the language barrier between them strikes Asala, she couldn't help but intrude and interpret, the soldiers allowed her to help and after the job was done, they treated her differently, They gave her clothes that differentiated her from the others, sat her at a table and asked for her help in communicating with her fellow refugees. As information gathered about each passenger on the Marine's ship before arrival, Asala felt useful.

It went from hunger & thirsts to awake after dark, having Italian pizza's with the Marines and their Captain while everyone else was asleep.

You don't know how lucky you are, Says the Captain to Asala.

I had to negotiate taking over your ship with the Libyan Marines. Says the Captain.

They were not far off from detaining you.

She knew that it could've been a different story, if it weren't for these Italian soldiers, she and all the other refugees on that boat would've been in the hands of the Libyans facing torture, extortion, enslavement or yet the unknown.

Let's not think about that! she thought the pizza in her hands was too good to worry about anything else!

Extract 4, Are we Home?

Reaching the land, Asala & her family had never seen news reporters before, She had never been given footwear, and she had never been asked so many questions before.

Taranto, Italy had given them warmth & a good night sleep before heading off to France for their final destination being the U.K.

We are almost there, this is real & this is happening, Says the father to his Family.

However, as they arrive in Calais, France by train and found themselves surrounded by immigrants camping patiently in the hopes of getting to the UK.

This is more than just us & our dream, I never thought there are so many of us out there, I never knew almost an entire nation could share the same hopes & dreams says Asala.

By Wednesday, the family had been camping for too long and were beyond tired and exhausted, they weren't sure if they would even make it to the UK.

Let's demand asylum in France Suggests Their eldest Asala.

By Friday night, taking matters into their own hands & applying for asylum in France, little did they know that in this part of the world, Friday nights, Saturdays, and Sundays were sacred days of the week, and none of the immigration bureaus would be open for shelter.

Two more nights, and this agony would end, Say's the father to his Family.

Nothing could be worse than being a castaway.

After two cold nights in a tent and lonely mornings, lack of communication because of the language barrier the family headed to the closest Bureau of Foreign Affairs in Calais, France.

Finally, The family asked for asylum. Within a few hours, they were sent to another town called Arras and as the family had settled into their new life in France, all three of the kids were enrolled in school, where they spent half of their day learning to read, write, and listen to French, Slowly but surely, they began to fit in with the other students and make friends.

A different outcome for their eldest daughter, Asala, was left behind due to her age, She was 17 at the time and had already graduated high school, unsure which grade to place her in, they decided to hold back her entrance application.

Despite the uncertainty,

I shall remain optimistic; I shall remain hopeful says Asala.

All she ever grew up hearing was the importance of education & what should she be titled in life...

As the family waited for their asylum application to be reviewed, the family received yet another letter, Efforts shattered, their application had been rejected, which meant they might be sent back to their home country

Knowing they came too far to give up, they fought the rejection and appealed in court.

When it came to preparing their appeal, they met people sitting behind a desk who were willing to listen, help, and provide everything and anything they needed, lawyers, interpreter and most importantly guidance for this chapter of their lives.

This is overwhelming Is it this humane in this part of the world...Murmurs the family amongst themselves.

When the part of the world they were living in was meant to be the kindest and warmest, and the religion everyone claimed to follow from where they came from seemed to be a mask for their dark intentions, coming all the way here started to seem right for these parents.

Handed a new set of anything they could possibly think of, from new clothes to shoes their size, toothbrushes and toothpaste, blankets, cotton sheets, and finally, a roof over their heads.

It was a dream come true at that point, a cosy little place until they settled in, while the French government decided their fate.

do we get to stay? Is this home? Says the Children to their Parent's.

This is not home yet,

Home is when we are together & know about each other's whereabouts yells their father in frustration!

All in good time, they received a letter with the court date.

They had to travel to Paris, where they faced three judges and an interpreter, they were interrogated thoroughly and their focus was on the father's life and his reasons for being in France and bringing his family all the to this side of the world.

Asala spoke up hoping to make a difference.

She spoke of her dreams for a better future, where she could experience liberty, fraternity, and equality like any other French citizen.

> *I want what everyone my age here on this land has, Says Asala,* Hoping her words makes an impact on the judges.

Months later, the family received the news they had been waiting for, In June of 2015 the family received a letter that changed their lives, The acceptance they were longing to have, The letter that brought with it fulfilled hopes and dreams of a new beginning.

They were granted residency in France, which meant they could decide where to live, which schools their children could go to and most importantly they finally had a piece of paper that helped them identify as a part of this country.

> *We belong, we belong, screams the children with joy!*

The family gracefully stayed in France, where all their children graduated from high school. They went on to

pursue their higher education bringing their father's dream to reality.

Extract 5, Do you speak French?

In a household where African traditions were cherished, the parents found themselves struggling to integrate into a French-dominated society. The father, adamant about his children returning home by 7 pm every day, hoped to preserve the family's values and morals, However Asala and her younger siblings longed for the freedom to spend time with their friends, Despite their protests the parents insisted on the importance of dinner as it was the only time they could sit and share their daily achievements.

One evening, as the children returned home from school, they were met with a traditional African cuisine, "Asida & Mullah," prepared by their mother.

Asala and her siblings, however, expressed their dissatisfaction and demanded food similar to what they were served in school.

Foie gras, Pâte à choux, or Quinche Lorraine.

The parents, frustrated with their children's disobedience, threatened to ground them if they didn't eat the traditional food and As the parents discussed their children's behaviour behind closed doors, they feared that their children were culturally detaching themselves & soon they wouldn't have anything in common with their Children.

The children's disobedience, refusal to eat traditional food, and constant commentary on their parent's behaviour were seen as signs that they were losing touch with their African roots, Is this the price we're paying, says their father each time he expresses his frustration with them.

The parents struggled to integrate, particularly due to the language barrier, as they were often discriminated against in the job market for lacking *"The power of communication"*.

I fear that my children would grow up feeling ashamed of their heritage and become disconnected from their culture"
says their mother.

On the other hand their mother's concern for her appearance was another battle a battle she only understood, particularly the cloth she wore around her head and her traditional clothing, was an added layer of complexity to the family's integration and as for their father a similar yet different battle that he only understood.

One day the father stands before the cashier, his eyes filled with weariness and frustration,

Do you speak English? Is this fresh baguette? Says their
father to the cashier.

NO! answers the French angerly!

He longs for a moment of connection, a bridge to cross the gap between himself and the unfamiliar world around him.

Instead, he is met with a language barrier that seems impossible to overcome.

The simple act of buying bread, once a routine task, has become a source of anxiety and tension, their father feels the weight of his family's expectations on his shoulders, knowing that each loaf he brings home represents a small victory in their struggle to build a new life in a foreign land,

As he stands there, struggling to find the right words, the father feels a sense of isolation that cuts deep.

He wonders if anyone truly understands the challenges he faces as an immigrant, the constant battles he fights just to be seen and heard, But even in the face of these obstacles, the father remains determined.

Deep down he knows that every moment of struggle is an opportunity to grow stronger, to learn new skills and adapt to a new way of life, he refuses to let the language barrier or cultural differences hold him back and instead chooses to face each day with courage and perseverance.

Leaves the store with his fresh baguettes in hand, the father feels a sense of pride and accomplishment, he knows that this small victory may seem insignificant to some but to him, it represents a triumph over the challenges of immigration and as he continues his journey, he carries with him the hope and determination to build a better life for himself and his family, no matter how difficult the road may be.

Alienation and Isolation is what these parents feel on daily basis, as they struggle to communicate effectively with those around them.

little did these children know it was more than just coming home with a baguette.

Extract 6, Unexpected Visitor!

A visitor, Asala, claimed to be her friend, a handsome Australian she had spoken to since she was only 13 years old.

I don't think this is a good idea, says her father, yet after days of convincing her father, the Australian finally lands in France and under this family's roof .

Asala felt like she knew him for years, Maybe it was those hours of small talk on social network, maybe it was just their destiny to finally meet.

His stay was only for 3 weeks and in those 3 weeks the Australian decided to propose, In their culture marriage is a sacred achievement for oneself and as for what Marriage meant for this Man, it meant commitment to the girl he called *"The Girl of his Dreams"*.

The Australian had planned the proposal of a lifetime for Asala, He whisked her away to the City of Love, Paris, and took her to the very top of the iconic Eiffel Tower.

As she stood there, surrounded by the breathtaking view of the city, he got down on one knee and pulled out a small, velvet box...

The anticipation was palpable as Asala's heart raced with excitement, The Australian gazed up at her with a look of pure adoration and said, Asala, I love you.

You have captured my heart in a way that no one else ever could,

Will you Marry me?"

Tears, streamed down Asala's face as she realized the magnitude of the moment.

All her struggles and hardships melted away in that instant as she looked into the eyes of the man, she knew was the one.

This girl, who was once homeless, identifies as Stateless with an unknown future and owning nothing but her words was being proposed to on one of the world's most admired monuments.

" I thought you would never ask, says Asala."

The Eiffel Tower seemed to radiate with joy and the stars above twinkled with delight.

Asala and the Australian embraced each other, feeling the world disappear around them, It was a moment that they would never forget, a moment that would forever be etched in their hearts and minds as the start of their journey together.

Extract 7, Love & Identity.

Asala's soon to be husband had to head back to Australia, and they both had unfinished plans including studies, work, and finances, they did not discuss who would be the one to leave their country of residence, who had to leave everything they knew behind.

Who would be the one to compromise.

As time went by, the 20-year-old became unsure about her decision, I am comfortable here, I don't want to leave if it ever came down to that, says Asala.

Do I really want to live in Australia?

I have never been, it seems like a faraway land, says Asala.

Regardless of the couple growing apart over the years, destined to be together, they found their way back to each other in 2018 when the Australian returned to France to plan their wedding, It was one of those things where her heart knew it's meant to be.

I believe he is the one, says Asala.

They happily celebrated their wedding with close friends and family.

A year later the first person from this refugee family applies for citizenship,

I am closer than I have ever been to an identity, says Asala.

She was close to a dream come true.

After sending off her application and waiting for two years, she received a mail that would declare her a lawful citizen of this land...

Efforts shattered,

We regret to inform you that your application for French citizenship has been denied. After careful consideration, we have determined that you are ineligible for French citizenship at this time.

The mail stated that she was not eligible for the French citizenship despite her 7 long years of integration and life in France, Everything that helped shape the young adult version of her, everything she has become & takes pride in, everything that she now identifies with was denied behind one reason.

She had married an Australian!

She understood the pain of rejection and what unexplainable heartache pain felt like.

She had to choose between love and identity!

What have I done wrong? Says Asala.

What have I missed?" Says Asala.

No one in her family understood what she was going through because the most important thing for this family was having a roof over their heads a refuge.

It didn't matter if they had identities or not or whether they identified to people as refugees or stateless, as long as they were legally eligible to call this place their lawful land of residence.

Anything that comes along is just a blessing.

With determination, she didn't give up and applied for another appeal yet the same rejection came along.

Is home where the heart?

or

Is home where my identity is? says Asala.

She arrived as a stranger But found a home in France.

For seven years she flourished, in her heart, it was a chance.

But then she found her love, Across the vast, open sea.

An Australian man she wed, and it felt so right, so free.

They built a life together, but her citizenship was denied.

A cruel choice she had to make, Between love and her French pride.

She felt like a refugee, Lost and alone in her own land.

Her heart torn apart, she cried, as she struggled to understand.

Why should love to be a barrier, To the home she's come to know?

She wished for acceptance and love, instead, she felt sorrow.

Oh, the pain of a refugee, forced to choose between heart and home.

May we open our hearts to all, and never let love be overthrown?

Extract 8, Sense of belonging.

Asala had to leave her family, unexpectedly, yet another integration she had to go through hoping it's her last.

As the world was in the grip of a pandemic, It has never witnessed before, Asala found herself feeling anxious about her relationship and the uncertainty of the future.

In a moment of desperation she decided without giving it much thought, *I must get into the next flight to Australia, says Asala...*

Fortunately, Asala had always been lucky and had been rescued from difficult situations in the past, the Australian Government had made it possible for family members to fly to Australia safely, despite the challenges posed by the pandemic.

As Asala arrived in Australia, she was filled with a sense of gratitude.

WELCOME HOME!

That's how the Australian's greeted her the minute she landed, She knew that she had made the right decision, She was relieved to be reunited with her Husband, She was grateful to the Australian Government for their support and assistance during this difficult time, and she looked forward to starting a new chapter of her life in her new home.

Love made everything a little easier, cultural barriers, cultural differences, and unfamiliar social norms.

Together they built a life for themselves in Australia,

With time Asala began to feel more and more at home in her new country and she was grateful for the love and support that had brought her there.

I want to work, study & make friends here, says Asala, I want to feel like a part of this country, says Asala.

As a Refugee she knew the struggle of feeling like not belonging to anywhere in the world, she knew the meaning to leaving Family & home behind everything familiar in the name of starting a Life.

The feeling of being uprooted can be overwhelming and isolating, as a result, the desire for a sense of belonging is strong.

The eagerness to be accepted, to feel like she is a part of a community, and to have a place to call home Leaving behind all that was known.

Starting anew life, feeling all alone,

A refugee's struggle, a daunting task, But Asala was determined to make it last.

With her partner by her side, she worked hard and never cried, Overcoming barriers, differences, and norms,

Building a life, weathering the storms

"I want to belong," Asala said,

To work, study, and make friends instead, A desire for acceptance, a yearning for home,

A place where she and her family could roam.

And in time, she found what she sought,

A sense of belonging, a feeling of thought,

A heart-warming story, a life well-made

In this new home, she found her place, A refugee no more, but a Human full of grace.

For her love and determination had conquered all, and she knew that her family's future would never again be small.

Extract 9, Miracle Baby.

Asala was overjoyed as she found out she was pregnant.

The idea of becoming a mother filled her with a mixture of excitement and fear, She wondered if she was ready for the responsibility of raising a child and if she could be as good a mother as her own.

As the couple prepared for the arrival of their baby. As the pregnancy progressed, Asala experienced all the usual physical and emotional ups and downs but throughout it all she remained focused on the fact that she was creating a new life and that knowledge gave her strength and purpose.

As the due date approached, Asala and her partner made all the necessary preparations, they attended prenatal classes, decorated the baby's room and eagerly awaited the arrival of their little one and when the day finally came, Asala held her newborn baby in her arms for the first time, she knew without a doubt that she was exactly where she was meant to be.

The love and responsibility that came with being Kaia's mother transcended any label or identity society could impose.

Kaia was born in Australia, bringing immense joy and relief. Asala knew that her baby's future was secure, and that she had nothing to fear for Kaia's life or identity.

"Kaia is safe," she whispered, *"Kaia is both blessed and a blessing, and nothing could possibly threaten the safety of this baby's life".*

Extract 10, Who are we?

From as little as owning a bed to a toothbrush to our clothes and things, to a community and culture, we leave behind everything we once called ours.

We are people who do not have anything that belongs to them, big or small, We have no place to call home, as we travel with a destination to the unknown.

We are willing to give up on our communities, our cultures, and our lifestyles in the hopes of finding a better place to call home, Unfortunately we are often perceived as aliens, simply because we represent everything that is different.

We have come to know persecution for reasons of race, religion, nationality, and political opinion,We do not know what freedom truly means or how it can be fully realized. Some of us have grown up in fear, constantly worrying about what tomorrow may bring, We cannot travel to any destination without being questioned and scrutinized.

Did we want to be identified as anything other than Human?

we wish to give ourselves our own label. We want what you have the ability to travel without being looked down upon, the freedom to live our lives without judgment or discrimination. We did not choose to leave everything behind, but we had to make this difficult decision in order to live rather than survive.

We are here now, in a new place, but we do not know if we truly wanted to be here, We want to start anew life, to build a new life for ourselves and our families, but it is not an easy road.

The pain of leaving behind everything we once knew is unbearable, and the uncertainty of our future can be overwhelming.

Who are we?

We spend the rest of our lives trying to find ourselves.

The challenges we face, We ask for compassion, kindness, and support as we strive to make a new home for ourselves in a world that can be hostile and unwelcoming.

We are the refugees, the displaced and the lost, Carrying only the memories of what we once called our home. Our hearts heavy with the pain of leaving behind Everything we knew, everything we loved all that we've known.

We walk through the unknown, with no destination in sight, Fearing the persecution that comes with being different and alone.

Our existence is reduced to a label, a burden to bear, A reminder of the intolerance and the hatred that we've known.

We dream of a life without fear or discrimination, A place where we can be accepted for who we are, Where we can rebuild our lives and our dreams, And leave behind the scars of our past, near and far.

But the journey is long, and the road is rough, With obstacles at every turn, and challenges to overcome.

The struggle is real, and the pain is deep, As we search for a place to call our new home.

Yet, amidst the pain and the hardship we face, We still hold on to the hope of a brighter tomorrow, With compassion, kindness, and support from those around us, We strive to heal, to grow, and to find ourselves anew.

So, let us stand together, hand in hand, And lift each other up with love and compassion, For we are the refugees, the displaced and the lost, In search of a home, a place of peace.